Poetry Through My Journey

Poetry Through My Journey

Me, Myself & God

Terry Catherine Potillo

Copyright © 2011 by Terry Catherine Potillo.

Library of Congress Control Number: 2011900114
ISBN: Hardcover 978-1-4568-4893-4
Softcover 978-1-4568-4892-7
Ebook 978-1-4568-4894-1

All rights reserved. No part of this book may be reproduced or transmitted in any form or by any means, electronic or mechanical, including photocopying, recording, or by any information storage and retrieval system, without permission in writing from the copyright owner.

This book was printed in the United States of America.

To order additional copies of this book, contact:
Xlibris Corporation
1-888-795-4274
www.Xlibris.com
Orders@Xlibris.com
84404

Contents

Acknowledgements 9
My Journey 11
I've Been Listening 13
The Prayer Garden 15
Rough Journey 16
Hey God.. 17
For God's Love 19
Weekend With Jesus 20
In Time 21
I Call It Beautiful.. 22
This Is Not What I Prayed For!... 23
Just Jesus... 25
Lead Me To The Rock 26
You Are The Love Of My Life 27
An Old Testament Trip 28
Soulmate Vs Playmate 30
Forever My Friend 31
What I Know 33
With Love To My Mc Family 34
Giving Thanks... 36
Love 37
The Lord Is My Shepherd.. 38
The Shepherd 39
Oh My God!.. 40
The Highs And Lows Of This Journey 41
Night Before Christmas With God 42
Happy Birthday Terry 43
Happy Birthday To Me 44
The Joy You Bring When Love Is The Key 45
God Said 47

Appreciation	48
When Love Is The Key	49
Fruit of the Spirit	50
Blessings	52
When I Can't Sleep	53
Hello God	54
Feeling God's Love	55
I'm Glad You Love Me	56
It's My Turn	57
I Can Hear You	58
Don't You Just Love It.!	59
Just For A Little While	61
Total Woman	62
Just Thinking	63
I Don't Mind Waiting . . .	64
Encourage Yourself	65
See Yourself In Your Future	66
Nobody But God	67
Praying, Praising & Packing	68
Here I Stand	69
Today	70
My Heart	71
It's My Time	72
Dont' Cry	73
My God	74
Tear Drops And Rain	75
Love Is Here	76
Letting Go	78
Why Be Bitter	78
Walking With God	80
God Is Enough	81
It's For Sale	82
House For Sale	83
Where Will I Go	84
I'm In Love	85
A House Is Not A Home	87
She's Still Family	88

Mama	88
At Last	90
Thank You Daddy	91
My Praise In Packing	92
I'm Ok	93
One Year Ago Today	94
Brand New Heart	95
Divine Downtime With God	96
How Do You Say Thanks?	98
Because He Loves Me	99
Feelings Just Feelings	100
Love Is The Key	101
Where's My Song?	102
Just Another Silly Love Poem	104
Little Girls And Pancakes	105
Little Girls	106
I Need You Lord . . . Right Now	107
A Grateful Heart	108
Show Me Lord	109
He Has My Heart	110
Only My God	111
Loving You	112
The Night Jesus Found Me	113
A New Home	114
Heaven Must Have Sent This	115
My Secret	116
This Is Where I Am	117
Feelings	118
LOVE FOUND	119
JESUS, ARE YOU HERE	120
If I Were not His	121
Keeping His Spirit With Me Through The Journey	122
February 19, 1923-November 18, 2001Eight Years Ago Today	122
Love Came, It's Time To Say Goodbye	124
Home Sweet Home	125
New Year New Joy	126
Just Thinking	127

THOUGHTS AND PRAYERS THROUGH MY JOURNEY

A Journey Through Thoughts and Prayers 131
Another Level of Glory 133
Thoughts of Thanksgiving 135
My Remarkable Journey 136
Merry Christmas Mc Family 137
I Am A Remarkable Woman 138
God's Love Is The Key 139
Update on God's Goodness 140
God And Bubble Wrap 141
My Journey 142
In Case I Don't See You . . . . Goodmorning, Good Afternoon &
    Goodnight . . . June 17, 2009 143
Friends~ Lovers~Marriages 144
A Smooth Transition 145
A Big Snow Storm Is Coming My Way 146
God And The Mailman 147
I'm Glad I Was Wrong 148

Acknowledgements

Thank you God, my creator, who knew I would have flaws. You created me, set me free, watched me grow and make many mistakes. You were there during my many defeats and celebrated my victories. I loved as if no one were watching, You heard me sing off key, I followed my dreams and I let some go. The list goes on. Your unconditional love kept going thought out this journey. Thank you God for speaking into my heart all hours of the night and giving me this opportunity.

To my Children, Aaron and daughter in love, Altangla and Noree, thank you for your support "Throughout the Journey" I LOVE YOU.

My Dad and Mom Howard and Catherine Potillo, Thank you for your unconditional love and support through the years. RIP Daddy. I hope I am still making you proud.

To my Big Sister Patricia, thanks for giving me a shoulder to lean on and encouraging me that I will be ok. Maxine, my baby sister(1953-2010), I'm glad I had the opportunity to read my poetry to you. Maxine was an enormous inspiration to me and my late night telephone buddy, I miss you so much. My Niece Tomika, thanks for all you help.

Special thanks to my Pastor, Bishop Walter S. Thomas Sr. Your Sunday sermons and Bible Studies have always encouraged and given me hope. Thank you Lady Thomas for your prayers. Candice Dickens, I thank God for placing you in my life for such a time as this, You helped me find "Terry". Stan & Carmelita Henson, thanks for adopting me for Sunday Breakfast. Thank you for your love, time and prayers. Thank you Marion Murphy for a loving place; Terry Williams for our girls night out; Vivian Harvey, you were always just a call away; Rev. Val Pearson and my Remarkable Sisters for your many cards and prayers; Valarie and Grant Murphy, for your time, prayers, encouragement and love. Thank You, Jan & Doug Vasilas, Denise McCray and Angela Smith. A special thanks to my "MC" Family; Rev. Terry Clark, Mike and Laura Espey for your fellowship, Stacy Ann Facey, Becky Sutherland, Denise Rossi, Jerry Webb,. Craig (KC Joe)

Livas and Margie Epps of The Kingdom Poets who encourage me to write and gave me a forum to share my poetry. Thank you to so many others who shared so much of their time, prayers and words of encouragement with me throughout my journey and many prayers for my sister, Maxine. I appreciate each and every one of you. "I Love You With My Whole Heart"

A very special thanks to Dr. Booker T. Anthony for your generosity to edit my first book. I truly appreciate you.

With all My Love . . . Terry

My Journey

J   Jesus was there right from the start
O   Only in His name I called
U   Under His care; we never part
R   Right on time with healing my heart
N   Never have I seen the righteous forsaken
E   Eternal love was His key
Y   Yes I know my God loves me

The Journey of Separation

On July 1, 2008, I started my journey into the unknown. One thing I knew for sure was that God had traveled on before me. He knew the rocky road that was ahead and all the emotions that were going to be felt. That is why he placed me on the sandy shores and carried me all the way.

I was on a roller coaster ride that just wouldn't stop. The love, comfort, peace and joy had slipped in every now and then and that's why I shouted and praised and sometimes found myself rolling on the floor. Soon I will be stepping into my new destiny. God knows when and where. I know He will be there also. It was a surprise to me but not a surprise to God.

During my separation a friend told me to write my journey through poetry. So here is a collection of my poems, prayers, thoughts, trials and triumphs through the months to come. This is my story of my journey of separation and divorce.

A Journey with Family and Friends

On July 18th I traveled south to see my family. It was the first time I've been on the road alone in many years. It was just me, myself and God. My first stop was Raleigh to visit my sister Maxine and then on to Durham for a visit with my son and daughter in love. Later I drove to Atlanta to see my baby girl in her showcase, my up and coming star.

I was making new memories on my new journey and I'm grateful for all of God's blessings, past and present and whatever His will for my future. I will be heading home soon not knowing what all lies ahead but knowing that God will be there as I navigate through my journey towards singleness.

I'VE BEEN LISTENING . . . . .

Listening . . . That's what I've been doing these last few weeks. Listening to God, listening to music, listening to advice, listening to praise reports, listening to prayers. Wow, have I've been listening. This is what I heard . . . .

Terry, This is God and I know you are going through
It was a big surprise to you but no surprise to me
This journey that you are on
I had to make you see.

There were things I tried to tell you.
There were things I wanted you to do.
But just like Jonah in the belly of the whale
You ran and pitched your sail.

Now that I have your attention
You're listening to me.
There are some things I need to say
So have a seat and be.

I have always loved you dearly
And I never left your side
I'm so glad that we could have this talk
And take this walk in stride.

I need you to be a witness
To those that come behind
And tell them of your journey
That God has made Divine.

Oh yes, I have been listening
To those words that's in my ears
But I'm so glad my Jesus
Has wiped away my tears.

09/12/2008

THE PRAYER GARDEN

Today I went to the garden to pray
I had to meet Jesus
There was so much to say.

I went to the Altar and fell on my knees
Tears streaming down my face
Knowing that my God was pleased
I had come into this place.

I prayed for healing for family and friends
My God knows what they need
I just kept praying and planting the seeds.

A spirit came over me while on bended knees
Asking God to intercede.
There's sickness in bodies with so much pain
I had to keep praying until healing was gained.

The garden was quiet; one other was there
I began to ask God to help her instead.
A Spirit came over me as I ended my prayer
Knowing that Jesus was standing there.

I stopped and gave thanks for the opportunity I had
In the Beautiful Garden of Prayer
Thanking God, Thanking Jesus
for taking me there.

Sept. 18, 2008

Rough Journey

My journey has been rough.
Dealing with the ups and downs
Of life can really be tough.
The loneliness alone is more than enough.
Being a Christian wife,
I didn't expect I'd have to deal with this kind of stuff.

I'm married, living single.
So I'm not at liberty to just go out and mingle.
Being married but separated.
It's hard to celebrate it.
At least until I am divorced.
So aloneness is my choice.

I spend most of my time in cyber space
But at the end of the day my home is just an empty place
Day after day that's the reality that I face
Yes I talk to people about it, the ones that I love.
And I know the Lord watches over me from above.
But it would still be nice to have someone to hug.

This is a hard journey I'm on.
Sometimes I don't even want to come home.
But that's what it's like when you build your life
With someone and then find yourself alone
I know I shouldn't complain
But that is one of the things that seem to ease the pain.
I tell you, this journey has me just about drain.

I've lost my appetite to eat.
Sometimes I cry myself to sleep.
So I just wait for the day when this is over
And I'm set free but until then
Will you all just pray for me?

HEY GOD

It's just me thinking about You.
Thanking You for all
You have bought me through.

Never missed a meal
A roof over my head
There's even a new Peace
When I go to bed.

Oh yes, and by the way
Thank you for the friends
Who call during the day
Just to say I Love You,
Just to say they care
Letting me know if I need them they'll be there.

Hey God
Thank you for bringing back my JOY
Giving me my Praise,
I couldn't ask for anything MORE.

Did I tell You that I Love You
Words could never say
The feelings that's inside of me each and everyday
I want everyone to see
Just how much You mean to me.

I'm glad that we are closer
Than We've ever been before
You never ever stopped Opening up doors.

One blessing after another
Giving me your cover
Holding on to this daughter never letting go
favor after favor and it really shows.

Hey God I'm leaning on Your promises
I'm leaning on My Faith
Because You've been so good to me
I'm in a really good place.
Hey God Thank You!

For God's Love

For Your love I'll do anything
With my heart I'll go anywhere
Telling folk how good You are to me
How on that fateful night you set me free.

For Your love I'll say everything
With my lips murmur the joy You bring
Praising, rejoicing and singing songs
While loving You all along.

For Your love I'll climb the hills
Taking with me your heart and skills
Letting everyone know from day to day
Trusting Jesus to lead the way.

For Your love I'll make the sacrifice
Always listening to Your Son's advice
Telling me He is the way to your heart
Showing God's Love right from the start.
For Your Love

Weekend With Jesus

I'm spending my weekends with Jesus
No other place I'd rather be
The quiet nights and the atmosphere
and I don't have to R.S.V.P.

It starts on Friday as I journey home from work
Telling me about the days to come
Letting me know right from the start
Yes we are gonna have some fun.

We talk about everything from A thru Z.
How the week has gone, no regrets you see
What to my amazing surprise
It's a wonder how He has opened my eyes.

It used to be a lonely time
People and places I couldn't find.
No one would call or come by to see how I am
But my Alpha and Omega
He just did it again.

I began to see my Destiny
And what my God wanted for me.
I'm just really glad He's in my life
Not just on weekends, but every night.

This I know for sure and it's an honor for me
Yes, my weekends with Jesus
Have set me FREE.

10-05-2008

In Time

This is not a good-bye
It's just a not right now
Some things just can't be
It's not God's Will you see.

Although it causes pain
That today we'll have to part
But know it won't be forever
Because you're always be in my heart.

Even though I Love You
It wasn't meant to be
I know one day you'll thank me
This is God's will you'll see.

So take the time to give Him Thanks
For not letting you have your way
You are His Child, I think you know
There will be another day.

And when the time is finally right
You'll know within your heart
All that you've been waiting for
God had it from the start.
I Love You Always.

10/12/2008

I Call It Beautiful

When I think of what God has made
My heart flutters with the care that He gave
Taking His time to make perfect the earth
For us to cherish the beauty and it's worth.

They say beauty is in the eyes of the Beholder
But who will deny the Art of the Father.
Whether its leaves turning red or yellow gold
There is a story of art being told.

The Beauty of His people all different shades
Only our God in heaven could have made
Our hair and eyes of different hues
All made beautiful for me and you.

I love looking at beautiful things
The beauty of the seasons, especially the spring
There's summer and winter and even the fall
I know God wants us to enjoy them all.

It's beautiful to see love in the air.
God ordained that with so much care
It's fragile and special what God had done
To be cherished and enjoyed by everyone.

So yes when I think of what God has made
He wanted to share it all, that's why He gave
All the beauty from shore to shore
All that beauty for us to adore.
I CALL IT BEAUTIFUL

10-13-2008

This Is Not What I Prayed For!

Lord this is me, in the prayer closet again.
I think You made a mistake my friend.
I didn't pray for this, it was not on my list.
Please can You make it go away.

I looked at it from all directions you see.
I left it at the altar and I can't comprehend this for me.
It's the wrong size and color for my life.
It's only going to cause me a lot more strife.

I won't take it home It won't fit in my car.
I don't even like how it looks so far.
Give it to someone else, maybe it's on their list.
This is not what I prayed for, You really did miss.

I'm going back on my knees to pray.
I hope you listen carefully to what I have to say.
My prayer list includes Peace, Love and Joy
So please don't give me what I did not ask for.

This thorn in my side, is for the roses not for me.
I'll keep praying until You set me free.
We had this talk before another time in my life.
This isn't what I prayed for not with all my might.

I'm on my knees it seems forever and a day.
I know You are listening to what I have to say.
I don't sleep at night, that's not news to You.
I thank You for patiently waiting until I am through.

After all the venting, after all the pleads
You keep giving me extra time down here on my knees.
I am here listening to what You have to say.
This is not what I prayed for, and, Oh by the way.

Lord you keep giving me extra time with You.
I am here listening to what You have to say.
Oh please Lord hear my prayer.
This is not what I prayed for.

The Peace and Joy You promised
Are they hidden in the clouds?
I'm down here shouting and talking really loud.
This is not what I prayed for.

What do You want me to say?
We have this conversation everyday.
I'm not going to stop praying and I'm not giving up
Because when this is all over I'll have another cup.

A cup filled with Blessing
My prayer of Peace, Love and Joy.
It will be running over with what I've been praying for
So today I'm Thanking You.
You have always seen me through.

This Is what I prayed For.
More peace, more love, more joy.
Thank You God, Thank You God.
THIS IS WHAT I'M PRAYING FOR.

10/13/2008

Just Jesus

Whether it's a trial you're going through
Or friends and people are leaving you
God is there, we know He cares.
The prayers and His comfort is in the air
Call on Him, Just Jesus.

A brand new house has just been blessed
The walls, the floors, the doors
Poured with oil, protected by Grace
Keeping you safe, till we meet Him Face to Face.
Call on Him, Just Jesus.

Our children in school are struggling too
To find themselves in this world.
Struggling to make the right choices is not new
Making tough decisions to worship you.
Call on Him, Just Jesus

Families torn apart worrying about everything
God will provide; the Angels sing
Working to make ends meet everyday
Trying to Praise Him along the way
Call on Him, Just Jesus.

It's in His name we'll find that peace
That God has promised praying without ceasing
Walking hand and hand with our Savior
Not letting go, holding on to His favor
Call on Him, Just Jesus.

The Lord is my shepherd
And I'm Trusting with all my heart.
For this is not my home to stay
I'm calling on Him, Just Jesus to lead the way.

10/17/2008

LEAD ME TO THE ROCK

Lord, there's so much going on in my life.
Sickness, division I'm overwhelmed with strife.
Sometimes I wish I could turn back the clock
Oh Lord, Lead me to the rock.

I've traveled this road before
Waiting for You to come and open doors
Watching the phone waiting for it to ring
Not knowing the news it would bring.
Lord, lead me to the rock.

Family is scattered all over the states
Not seeing them regularly my heart cannot take.
I watched them grow into the adults that they are
Never thinking they would move so far.
Lord, lead me to the rock.

A heart that's overwhelmed
A mind sometimes bound
Wondering what my God is up to
When is this all going to be through.
Lord, lead me to the rock.

Lord You are my solid rock
Can't turn back the clock
There's nothing new under the sun.
We know Your will, will be done.
Lord, lead me to the rock.

You are the firm foundation for my life
Keeping me on the path You know is right.
You are my solid rock and my salvation
My strong foundation my solid rock.
Lord, lead me to the rock.

10/26/2008

You Are The Love Of My Life

Talking to me everyday
Knowing the right words to say
I'm listening very tentatively.
Jesus, You are the Love of my life.

The night You found me
The things You let me see
Holding me close to Thee
Not letting me go but yet setting me free.

The Angels sang their song
As we made our journey along
Getting a glimpse of my Destiny
The amazing future You have for me.

Jesus, You are the Love of my Life
Your Grace and Love sustains me through the night
You have taken away my pain, Replaced it with pure joy
Now my light shines for You.

Yes Jesus, my light shines because of You.
You made my journey easy to go through
Sending love, support and encouragement
I'm sharing my testimony while giving You the Glory.
You are the Love of my Life.
My True Love Story.

10/31/2008

An Old Testament Trip

God created the World you see
So Adam and Eve could come to be.
They lived in a garden with many fruit trees.
One day they ate and were forced to leave.

Noah was obedient and built the Ark
Collected the animals so they could start.
For forty days and nights the rain came,
God sent a Rainbow and said never again.

Moses went to the Mountain, He had to go away.
The Lord came to him, Told him what to say.
Up there he saw a Burning Bush
Came down again with The Ten to push.

There was no water for the people to drink.
The crops also withered and started to shrink.
Moses took the staff in his hand,
Spoke to the Rock as God commanded.
The Rocks cried out
With water, no Spout
The people drank, didn't understand
Along with the animals, the plants, it was His plan.

Joshua led as he was told
Serving God as a whole household
Making it to the Promise land
They buried him there as the story stands.

Naomi has a story to tell
Two widow daughters-in-law, what now
Orpah went on her own little way
While Ruth clung to Naomi, it was a brand new day.

Job was chosen to test his faithfulness.
Sickness invaded his body, he lost everything
But he never cursed God and so to the end
Received his blessings; God found favor in him.

My story goes to the Potter's House.
I saw Him working all day and night.
It was me I saw up on that wheel
Shaping and molding I couldn't keep still.
I saw my flaws they were visible you see.
The Potter was reshaping me.

Daniel prayed to the only one God he served.
Making the King mad he thought how absurd
They threw him in the lion's den to die.
God locked their jaws and Daniel did rise.

I'm ending my journey into another time
When Jesus was born and I accepted Him as mine.
On a cross one day He died for our sins.
Let's give him the Glory; Eternal life begins.

11/10/2008

SOULMATE VS PLAYMATE

Sitting here all alone
Thinking about Jesus you should have known.
I wonder what He's doing to me.
My thoughts have strayed; please set me free.

Your heart and mind is a playground, open to all.
Don't let them in or you will fall.
Call on His name everyday.
Keep those playmates farther away.

This is your season for you to shine.
Don't lose your favor, Stay Divine.
They mean you no good with all of their game.
Don't let them take you back to shame.

So guard your Heart with your entire might.
Always keep God in sight for this fight.
You'll never know when they will appear
So keep your praise and salvation near.

11/11/2008

FOREVER MY FRIEND

The day you came into my life
Things were hectic and full of strife.
You read my story, gave God the glory.
It was the beginning of Forever my friend.

You encouraged, prayed and were always there
Telling me of Jesus' love and that life's not fair.
You listen and spoke of God's own words
Trying to comfort me no matter the herds'.

You inspired me to write through all my pain
Dried my tears with laughter and
Sent inspirational prayers throughout the day
While I gathered my thoughts along the way.

And when the night came and I couldn't sleep
I looked out there and saw your face.
You were there for me through thick and thin.
God choose you for this I know within.

My heart can't thank you enough today
For helping me see a clearer way
To Gods favor and love behold.
God is my Love I've been told.

You'll always be my forever friend
Helping me on this journey till the end.
I'll ask God to bless you really good
For being the forever friend who understood.

I love you yesterday today and forever as
A friend who came during my endeavor
And pulled me out of despair.
I'm so glad God sent you there.
I Love You
My Forever Friend.

11/20/2008

What I Know

God is keeping me safe and sound
No matter what seems to come around.
He's taking me to new places.
It seems He knows just what I'm facing.

God has been listening to my prayers
Telling me He has always been there.
Even when my faith was weak
He knew just when to speak.

God has His loving arms around me
His Comfort and Spirit for all to see.
This transformation came with a price
But everything from God is worth the sacrifice.

God is speaking to me and I can hear
For there was a time I had closed my ears.
I can't wait for our conversations now
Because I know all His advice is sound.

God has promised love and peace.
I will not disappoint Him my faith has increased.
I'm going to stay with Him on this journey of mine
Because I know this is my time.

11/22/2008

With Love To My Mc Family

    I am so blessed to be able to spend this Thanksgiving with my son, daughter, daughter in love, my sister Maxine and my extended family here in North Carolina. Today as my family gives thanks before dinner I also give thanks to God for my MC Family.

I never thought in my wildest dreams
That I would find my friends in space.
I thank God for bringing me to this place.
A place where love have lived
Among the many pages of blogs.
I never thought I'd meet so many
Sharing their love.

Sometimes we get too serious on things we have to say.
Other times, our comments seem to get in the way.
The way God wants us to respond
With loving caring words
Lets give Him thanks and show His love
As we receive our blessing from above.

This Thursday is set aside for all to share a meal
To give God thanks for everything.
Let's not let the devil steal
The joy that's coming to visit you
On this Thanksgiving Day.

Let's keep the thanks and praise flowing in the air
Telling God you're glad He is the center of this day.
And when all the family and friends have gone on their way
Fall on your knees and say a prayer
For the fellowship you just shared.

Oh Yes, we have a lot to be thankful for
This Thursday I know for sure.
But let everyday be a day of Thanksgiving
Showing God's love forever more.

11-25-2008

GIVING THANKS

It's Thanksgiving Day, November 27, 2008. Today before dinner we share what we are thankful for.

To my Mom, sisters and family, I am thankful that God choose us to be a family. I love you. I'll choose you again and again.

To my Pastor and church family, Rev. Val Pearson and my Remarkable Sisters, I love you so much.

My MC Family and to those I have a bond with and to my circle of friends there, I love you. Thanks for all your comments, supporting my poetry and blogs, prayers and your love. I am so grateful for all of you.

Thank you for the sun that shines.
Thank you for the love that's mine.
Thank you for the birds that sing.
Thank you God for everything.
Amen.

LOVE

Sharing this feeling is what we must do
Giving it to the ones we trust
Hoping that they do right by you
Reading God's words to find the clue.

Spreading the joy that's carried inside
Seeing the fruits of the labor arrive
Knowing you have done the best you could
While doing God's work like we should.

Saving the best you have to give
Keeping it and hoping that love will live
Inside the heart so hard with fear
You won't even let Jesus come near.

Faith, hope and love are designed
To give and release and to feel divine.
Faith is what we have to serve God.
Hope for the future is keeping it alive.

But the greatest of these is love
Sent from heaven on the wings of a dove
Not to take for granted nor to be in vain
But to share and nurture and return the same.

They say love starts at home
Giving you something to call your own.
Taking it out to the people you'll meet
Knowing it's in God's plan to be meek.

So if this love is special to have
Shouldn't everyone be feeling grand
Glowing and showing how the Lord provides?
All this love you can't keep inside.

The Lord Is My Shepherd

It's three thirty in the morning and I just love how He wakes me up and gives me words that comes together with praise, Thanking Him for everything and knowing no matter what I am *still* in His Arms. TO GOD BE THE GLORY.

The Shepherd

Psalm 23

I needed His guidance in every way
Taking me along this path to stay.
Could have, would have wasn't a choice
Hearing His powerful and almighty voice.

I haven't wanted for anything.
He supplies all my needs with all He brings
Down on my knees to Him I pray.
He restores my soul each and every day.

I'm walking through this valley and I have no fear
Because my God is forever near.
His arms are around me giving comfort to my life
My enemies are fleeing right out of my sight.

He's prepared me for this journey
And anointed me with peace.
His goodness and love are all over me
My life was a gift you see.

I am dwelling in His promise all the days of my life.
Giving Him praise and honor, I will never part
Holding Him close for this brand new start.
Yes, The Lord is My shepherd and
I love Him with all my heart.

12/18/2008

Oh My God!

Oh my God
I Love You
With all my Heart.
I do love you my God.

My God I need you.
Come and hear my prayers.
Tonight I'm here for you.
I love you my God

Oh my God, I do love you.
Loving You is easy.
There's no demand I face before your Grace.
Oh my God I love You, I love You,
Oh my God

Yes I do love You my God.
I will praise You with all my soul.
I will praise You today.
I know it's the only way to you my God.

I love You, Yes I do love You today.
My God You are healing in a mighty way.
My soul gives you the honor.
My God is awesome everyday.

How You have made a way for me.
I love you more and more.
Oh my God, I love You, yes I do.
Love You today in every way.

Loving You is the only way I know.
My God, my God
I love You, oh my God.

12-19-2008

THE HIGHS AND LOWS OF THIS JOURNEY

It's December 20, 2008. I know we wish we could predict our future, well maybe not too far ahead but just in the hours ahead. Today I feel like that. I just had the most not so good two weeks ever. I know God is in control and for every little twist and turn I believe it is His will.

I pray and say to myself that in five minutes it will be better and most of the time it is, but when it isn't one moment seems like eternity. If I never had a problem how would I know my God could solve them and so today I thank Him for this not so great moment because I know this too will pass.

Since I've been on this journey I have some caring family and friends who have been on my Roller Coaster Ride with me. It hasn't been easy and some days I can't tolerate myself. There are sometimes when I myself don't understand what God is doing and it's at those times I need my God, family and friends the most. No, it's not easy but this is where I am and I thank-you for being here with me.

NIGHT BEFORE CHRISTMAS WITH GOD

It's December 24, 2008, Christmas Eve and I've been listening and talking with God. I would like to share a little of our conversation.

"Terry," He said, "You are my special daughter and I love you very much. Yes, it's almost Christmas and I'd like you to think about all the gifts you have received this year." Well I thought about it long and hard and then I said . . . . "God, the best gift I have received this year was You. A turn of events in my life has bought me closer to you than I have been in a long time. In fact God, I thought for awhile you had forgotten all about me down here." He replied "NEVER." I went on to tell Him, "God, you told me not to worry about food, clothes. Yes Matthew 6:25, I know that scripture." And then I went on to tell Him, "God, you have supplied all my needs on this journey and that is the greatest gift. Thank you so much. Oh and before I go God, You sent me the best friends in the whole wide world. Yes I got all these new friends and some old ones from the neighborhood are calling, WOW, Thanks God. You are awesome. One more thing God, The Gift of Jesus, You just keep giving and giving and giving and for that I want to say THANK YOU LORD FOR ALL THE GIFTS YOU HAVE GIVEN ME, not just this year but for everyday that I have been on this earth." Then God whispered. "The greatest of these is LOVE." "Oh Yes, 1 Corinthians 13; 13" I replied "THE GIFT OF LOVE"

What was your greatest Gift this Year?

HAPPY BIRTHDAY TERRY

December 26, 2008

It's your 58th birthday
The celebration of your very first day
Before you had a clue
When life was oh so new.
Your child like spirit reflects the many things
You wish you could still do.
Your beauty reflects how good life has been to you.
Your loving personality holds the truth.
So with glasses held high let's all salute.
May this birthday be the best one yet
And all that you prayed for I hope that you get.
I know that you truly deserve it.
Happy Birthday
Happy 58th Birthday Terry.

Happy Birthday To Me

I was told that no one will come to a party the day after Christmas so I had ice cream and cake with my three sisters and sometimes cousins. As I grew up it was the same thing, ice cream and cake with my family. In December of 2000, I was turning fifty and wanted to have this big party. I planned, shopped, sent out invitations and the worst happened. After a major snow storm a Huge rain with over three feet of water filled the basement family room. I cancelled my party and was surprised with a birthday dinner at a local restaurant.

Yesterday, December 26, 2008, was my 58th Birthday and I gave myself a party and guess what? People came. It was more than ice cream and cake with my sisters. I played music from the 60's and 70's and yes I even sang. I want to take this time to thank my family and friends for coming to my party. Last night after my family left, I went back and read all my birthday cards and comments from my MC family and was overwhelmed by the greetings. It truly Blessed my Heart. Celebrating my first birthday on my new journey towards a new destiny with so many family and friends was truly a blessing.

The Joy You Bring When Love Is The Key

Gentle was your voice speaking
Telling me all about the God I was seeking
How to live for Him everyday
Nothing but peace showing me the way.

Wise beyond your years I thought
Not to mention the joy you brought
Holding the key to my heart I gave
No expiration, my love I would save.

We were on line chatting every night
Sharing and reading our poems we did write
Reaching out to each other for what was missing
Not knowing it was something we were wishing.

Two people looking to fill a void
All the while talking about the Lord.
A love we know could never be
No expiration, You still have my key.

This gentle voice somehow calmed my tears
Talked to me about letting go of my fears.
Fears to Trust and Love again
I know some day this will have to end.

Forever friends we will always be.
I think that's what God intended for me.
A friendship full of respect and love
That could have only come from above.

You have become my on line love
In my wildest dreams I float like a dove.
You will never be pushed out my heart, you see.
Loving you is what our Friendship means to me.
I LOVE YOU

Thank you for being on my journey. Sometimes it wasn't easy but you stayed and that's true friendship, true love. I appreciate you and all you have shared with me. You are my forever friend and I Love You.

January 18, 2009

GOD SAID

You know that I've been listening
To everything you say.
Brighter days are here right now.
Wow! It is a brand new day.

You said you'll never leave me.
That promise you kept true.
I love the time I'm spending
Just to get close to you.

God, you told about the love
I am receiving now.
It is for me to cherish.
It's real and it is sound.

You said it takes some rain.
And you added lots of sun.
It's needed to make the rainbows
That make my life real fun.

God, you said over and over
How much you love this child
Holding me in your arms so tight.
God you said with all your might.

So God I'm hearing you very clearly.
I'm so glad your voice is so near.
You said enjoy this journey my dear.
God, your voice is always sincere.

Thank you God, you are so Amazing
I HEAR YOU.

01/15/2009

Appreciation

Tonight I sit here thinking about you
About my journey and all I've been through.
How you were here cheering me on
Telling me about a new days dawn.

I'm glad you are on this path with me
Holding the key and letting me be free.
Free to shed some tears and thoughts
And giving and sharing wisdom you bought.

I appreciate you
More than you'll ever know.
If I could tell God how you helped me through
I know He will have the biggest crown for you.

I pray one day she will see the Light
and know how precious you are in God's sight.
And maybe the fire that used to burn
She'll have the desire and love will return.

So you keep on writing and encouraging
And soon one day you will be inheriting
The love and joy you so rightly deserve
Abundance of Blessings you'll have to reserve
From my Heart

01-19-2009

When Love Is The Key

My journey has shortened and a new one has begun.
God sent his Angels with energy and fun.
Beside me they did abide
Never missing was Jesus inside.

The road sometimes was hard for me to bear
But the Angels keep pushing,
Telling me, "You're gonna get there.

2009 we are increasing the Faith
Time spent with God you have to make.
Moving mountains is the only choice
Very clearly hearing God's voice.

Unconditional love I keep reading in blogs.
Mike even talked about our "First Real Love."
This journey was made easier for me.
I know it was the Angels God sent, you see.

It's all through the Bible for us to read
"LOVE IS THE KEY" FOR YOU AND ME.

01/22/2009

Fruit of the Spirit

Galatians 5: 22-23

Love is patient, love is kind.
Make sure you don't leave this one behind.
It's the greatest I was told
And I know this one is good for the Soul.

Joy is what God gives you they say
Don't let the world take it away.
This joy you have is a gift from God.
They can't steal it, it's stronger than the rod.

Peace, in your world is more precious than gold
No matter what you've been told.
Hold on to your peace today.
Let no man come and take it away.

Patience is a treasure in your chest
When you have it you are at your best.
God has it for us unconditionally.
Patience is what we needed spiritually.

Kindness is what the world can use.
Too many are being abused.
Show it to a stranger to make their day.
You have so much inside just give it away.

Goodness surely it's in the 23rd Psalm.
It comes with Mercy and Goodness brings it along.
Surely Goodness and Mercy I must say
Because of what God is doing today.

Faithfulness, Great is Thy faithfulness.
God does not take a rest.
He continues to use it and we are blessed.

Gentleness comes with the softness we share
Letting others know how much we care
Loving and encouraging at our best
Don't let your gentleness take a rest.

Last but not least is self-control
Never let this one out of your soul.
To lose this is falling out of His Will
Compromising God's Favor, Just be still.

There we have this big bowl of fruit
Controlling our lives for us to produce.
Keep it very close to your heart.
Never ever let your fruit depart.

January 24, 2009

BLESSINGS

God gives us many blessings,
More than we will ever need,
Some are wrapped in pretty paper,
Some started from a seed.

There's blessings that comes into our Hearts
Coming from God right from the start.
These Blessings come to make us feel
That we are all a part,

A part of God's special family.
Blessing others so they can see.
The love that comes from these blessings
Is also for you to set yourself free.

When we count our Blessings
It's hard to ignore
The many times He's opened doors,
Doors that were always closed before.

I don't always appreciate my blessings.
Yes, I'm guilty of that too
But when I think of how good He's been
In my life and everything I do,

I fall on my knees and start to pray,
Lord forgive me for what I didn't say.
Thank you God for all my blessings
That you have sent me every day.

January 27, 2009

WHEN I CAN'T SLEEP

When I can't sleep I talk to God
Telling Him about my day
Although He knows everything
He's listens to what I have to say.

There are things I say to Him at night
I would not want Him to bring to the light.
He keeps my secrets to Himself you know
I am so glad to Him I go.

There are times during our conversation
I'll have this moment when I can't stop
Telling Him how grateful I am.
Fighting my Battles until the end.

Sometimes we talk all night long
And when morning comes I am strong
Strong enough to face my day
Knowing no sleep I had He's made a way.

When I can't sleep and come on-line
There's not too much peace I find.
Going back to read the word I left behind
Is the only joy that will ease my mind.

I'm so glad to know
That I have this place to go
And every time it's God I find
Giving me this peace of mind.

When I can't sleep instead of counting sheep
I call on Him and we go deep
I meet Him face to face
And He takes me to this joyful place.

When I can't sleep I know now
It's Jesus who comforts His sheep.
Because the Lord is my shepherd
He restores my soul every time we meet.

Hello God

I'm glad you stopped by today
So many things were getting in my way
Trying to stop my blessings from you,
Trying to keep my joy from getting through.

I know I serve this awesome God.
His promises are my lighting rod,
Keeping me safe in the storms of my life,
Removing all this unnecessary strife.

The time we had today was so surreal
I can feel the places that were healed.
My body and mind have been under attack
And you told Satan just get back.

Your Word holds true for those seeking it.
My best friend said please don't quit.
Keep thinking positive, get back in His spirit.
Move those mountains; God can cure it.

I am making you this promise so I won't miss
My desire to be in your presence, I will insist
That no matter what I will walk the straight and narrow
Until You come again, my eyes are on the sparrow.

FEBRUARY 3, 2009

FEELING GOD'S LOVE

I'm feeling the love God promised me,
Spreading it around the world to see.
People are asking what is this love.
All I can tell them is it comes from above.

I'm feeling the love of my children.
God's gift from heaven, that's my key.
Calling and texting when they are free.
Sending much love and hugs to me.

I'm feeling the love of family,
The one God chose to be with me.
There's dinner's and fun for everyone,
Spreading our love from daughter's to sons.

I'm feeling the love from all my friends,
Sharing our hearts there is no end,
Forgiving and giving unselfishly
Unconditional love from you to me.

All over the universe and across the seas—
North and South, East and West
Just like God giving us His best.
Love is the key—you know the rest.
WE ARE FEELING GOD'S LOVE.

FEBRUARY 5, 2009

I'm Glad You Love Me

On a chilly night in February
My heart is warm as can be.
I have this wonderful Savior
And I'm glad that He cares for me.

As He walks with me on this journey,
Giving me directions that's in His will,
Telling me that I'm doing good
And how to stand and be still.

I'm glad you love me Jesus.
Others have left on this race.
It's You that have me in this place.
Determination is what saves my face.

Your Word I have hidden in my heart.
I'm careful never to let it part.
Someday this will all be explained.
Until then I will trust you and remain.

I'm glad that You love me Jesus.
To every beginning there is an end.
I'll press on until I finish this race
For your Love I will not have to defend.

So on this chilly night with this clear blue sky
I'm not sitting around waiting to die.
I'll live my life to the fullest, that's my destiny.
And there's no other man I'd rather be with
Than you. Jesus, I'm glad you love me.

February 13, 2009

It's My Turn

It's my turn
To be all that I can be.
I know that it's my Jesus
That's looking out for me.

I thought I needed you
Every second of my day
But all it only taught me
That Jesus was the way.

It's my turn.
Love is all around.
I was looking in all the wrong places
When Jesus I found.

You don't know the oil
In my Alabaster Box
But my Lord and Savior
Is all I care about.

It's my turn.
This little shining star
Is making Jesus very proud
Even from afar.

You were not there
When I needed you most,
But I tip my hat because you always knew
It was Jesus only that would get me through.

It's my turn
To let my light shine.
All the love He's had for me
Has always been mine.

February 14, 2009

I Can Hear You

I hear you loud and clear
Sending blessing in my ear.
I hear the wind, the laughter.
I can even hear the joy I'm after.

I hear you when you're crying.
Your tears both joy and pain,
The laughter that you once knew
Will soon be back again.

I can hear you from across the seas
Telling the world how it should be.
The voices of victory is near
Spreading the Good News we hold so dear.

I can hear you God, loud and clear
Like a deer panting for the water.
Hide this in your heart, my precious daughter,
Listening to the cries of the slaughter.

I can hear you no matter where I go.
It is His plan; now take your seeds and sow,
Wanting it to be heard around the world
That Jesus Christ is Lord. Yes, I am His girl.

02/15/2009

Don't You Just Love It.!

The smell of the air after the rain
Riding on a train
Feeling the wind on your face
Knowing all about God's Grace.

Don't you just love it
Hearing kids laughter
Knowing what you are going after
Following your dreams

Strolling through the park
Seeing a sunset over the hills
Doesn't it give you a trill?
Knowing God's art is still.

Don't you just love it
Knowing how Great our God is?
He's just giving us his love
Unconditional from the start

Seeing the smiles on their face
As we walk through the door
Just asking for more.
How was your day.

Don't you just love it
When the telephone rings
And the voice on the other end sings
"Hello, I was thinking about you."

Meeting new friends
Reconnecting with old ones
It's ok that your work is never done.
Don't you just love it.

Love knowing that victory is yours
Opening new doors
Things you've never seen before
Knowing that with God He has more.
DON'T YOU JUST LOVE IT.!

02/16/2009

JUST FOR A LITTLE WHILE

Just for a little while
I have to say goodbye.
So many friends are here
That's very special and dear.

Just for a little while
I have so much to do.
I'm really going to miss
Spending time with you.

Reading all the blogs you write
encouraging other to stay bright
Walking in faith, moving mountains too
Saying goodbye is what I have to do.

Just for a little while
With all I have to do
It's hard to sit here every day
Knowing other things are in the way.

So just for a little while
I'll say goodbye to you
Forever in my heart you know
I will return; now I really have to go

02/17/2009

Total Woman

Total woman. That's what I am.
Because of God's love I have from within
His Grace has sustained me in the darkest of days.
I know it's because I'm following His ways.

The Road was made clear from the Word I did read.
His precious Son on the cross He did bleed
Because of His love I have eternal life
Nothing in this world is going to cause me strife.

I'm a total woman and it is well with my soul.
God has taken away all of the old
Transforming me into the Woman He say.
I'm determined to stay and continue to pray.

I know there's more work for the Lord to do.
We all know that He isn't through
Making me wonderfully and fearfully too.
Yes, I'm the total woman, waiting for you.

February 24, 2009

JUST THINKING

If all the world were happy
And no one ever cried
Always smiling always cheerful
And no one ever died.

If everyone had food to eat
And hunger were no more
Spending days just greeting
And very little chores.

If every day were sunshine and never any rain
And there will be no ice or snow
And flowers will sit on every window pane
And everything would grow.

If every heart were full of love
And there were never any hate
I know that there would be a crowd
At the heavenly pearly gates.

I'm just thinking how I would like to see
All the world around me to finally be
What I think God created that day.
Why don't we just let Him have His way?

02/28/2009

I Don't Mind Waiting . . .

If I'm in a hurry I'll stay at home
No need to stand in those lines alone.
I don't mind waiting with my thoughts you see.
It's all about God and what He's done for me.

I don't mind waiting for the seasons to change.
I have so much to do so much to rearrange.
It's the patience that's tested as I wait on Him
But I know in my heart what is coming at the end.

I don't mind waiting for the Lord.
You see, it's in His time no need to get bored.
There's so much to do while I'm waiting on Him.
I know He has something special for this rare gem.

I don't mind waiting; I'm gonna stay in this race.
I know God has my best interest in this place.
I'm waiting on Him; no place I'd rather be.
My reward is His face I know I'm gonna see.

I don't mind waiting on the Lord.

March 3, 2009

ENCOURAGE YOURSELF

When dark clouds seem to hover over you
Everything in your life seems really blue.
Don't believe the devil; he is a liar.
Encourage yourself in the Lord.

Not enough time in your busy day?
Look to the Lord to make a way.
Count on Him in all you do.
He is always here to see you through.

People disappointing you running out of your life.
There's a reason, let them go, you don't need the strife.
Open up your heart to God; He is all you need.
Their season is over; go and plant new seeds.

Encourage yourself; stay focused on Him.
Be patient and wait and see what He sends.
The world is full of loving people; they're not far.
Never forget you are God's Shining Star.

March 5, 2009

Terry Catherine Potillo

SEE YOURSELF IN YOUR FUTURE

Our God is amazing with everything He touches.
He shows us His love which we know is very much.
Always opening doors making plans for us
He sees us in our future; praising Him is a must.

We don't know what the future holds
But let's live today like we will grow old.
Our kids are dying young; parents don't know what to do
Grieving for their loss thinking why am I going through.

I see you in your future; eternal life is what I see
But you have to get your life right; Jesus is what you need.
We don't know the day the time or the hour.
God has given you and me all of this power.

How are you going to use the gift that He gives?
God sees you in your future. How are you going to live?
You can't serve two masters; you have to make a choice.
There's not much to think about when you hear God's voice.

Will you listen or will you turn away?
Will you believe or will you lose your faith?
No one is perfect; we all make mistakes
but sincerely repent and you shall see his grace.

03/10/2009

NOBODY BUT GOD

Nobody but God loves me as He does.
Caring, gentle and always seeing me through
Being with me every step of the way
Coming just to brighten my day.

Nobody but God can dry my tears
Coming in the night to calm my fears
Wrapping me in his loving arms
Keeping me safe from all harm.

Nobody but God has put this smile upon my face
Giving me his word offering me His Grace.
Promise after promise and He's never failed
Telling me the gates of hell will not prevail.

Nobody but God will get me to the finish line
On this journey He's been here all the time.
Sometimes when I couldn't get a prayer through
It was Jesus that told me "God has never left you."

Nobody but God is Here for you too
Loving and guiding us all the way through.
Your destiny is not very far off by the way.
Just keep him close and praise Him every day.

March 17, 2009

Praying, Praising & Packing

Yes, I've been praying everyday
About the move that's coming my way.
God and I have been busy in here
Taking away my greatest of fears.

Oh, I've got my praise on too.
There is still so much we have to do.
The yard sales are continuing this week
Praising Him for the guidance I seek.

And I'll never forget the packing that's done
All the while God and I are having fun
And when I get weary and tired too
He gives me this energy to get through.

Praying and praising and packing today
God and the bubble wrap keep making a way
Helping me to forget my sorrows and take flight
Taking my joy to a brand new height.

Thank you God it's not always easy.
I'm so glad you are here keeping me busy.
I don't know what I would do without you
Keeping me from getting totally blue.
Thank you God for seeing me through.

March 18, 2009

HERE I STAND

I stand before you oh Lord
Telling you about my day.
There is so much I want to say oh Lord
but you already know my way.

I need you here here right now.
I'm having these feelings of being overwhelmed.
It's at the Rock you are leading me.
It's your face I need to see.

Here I stand in need of your mercy.
Send it with grace and peace.
Your word I am reading is in my heart.
I will never ever let it part.

It's me, It's me and you oh Lord
In this garden of prayer.
I just want to know just how long
Will I have to be there.

Hear I stand
Hand in hand
Holding on to you oh Lord.
Never let me go.

March 19, 2009

Today

Today, I will praise God
From where He's brought me thus far.
Never once did He leave me
Making sure His Love I see.

Today, I'm truly blessed.
Despite all my years of mess
Forgiveness He's given me
On this journey setting me free.

Today, His mercy surrounds
Keeping me from feeling overwhelmed.
Grace is on my plate also
Keeping me where ever I go.

Today I'm feeling His power.
There's so much to do in the coming hours
He's given me the strength to endure.
I am feeling Him for sure, for sure.

Today, nothing but Peace in my space.
I am looking only into His face
Asking for guidance along the way
Today, He has the only say.

TODAY AND EVERYDAY HE'S SHOWING ME THE WAY.

March 28, 2009

My Heart

My heart belong to Jesus
And I'm not giving it away
Just to anybody
Who has so much to say.

I'll guard it with The Word
And all my armor too.
Jesus will protect it
From all it's going through.

Sometimes it on my sleeve
For others to abuse.
Then Jesus came beside me
And said it will not be used.

My heart beats very gentle
With a softness all it's own.
When Jesus thinks it's ready
He'll send it out on loan.

This Heart of mind will be ready.
Someday I know it will
But Jesus still can keep it safe,
Sheltered until it reaches The Pearly Gate.

March 31, 2009

It's My Time

It's my time.
I will shine
With God's Love
sent from above.

It's my time.
I'm claiming what's mine.
God said yes.
He always wants my best.

It's my time.
It's my destiny.
It's my time.
I'm just fine.

It's my time.
If you are going through
Only God will do
What He promised to.

It's my time.
I'm not looking back.
God has set the track.
He's taken up all the slack.

It's my time.
Can't you hear the shout.
All of you know
What this is all about.

IT'S MY TIME!!!!!!

March 31, 2009

Dont' Cry

Why so many tears.
Didn't God say he will
Calm your fears?

Why so many tears?
Cast all your concerns
For God really cares.

Why so many tears?
Just sing a song of praise,
Don't you know God hears.

Why so many tears?
This battle is the Lord's.
He is fighting for you my dear.

Why so many tears?
Why such a heavy heart?
God had your back right from the start.

APRIL 8, 2009

My God

My God has not forsaken me.
Some things He leaves for me to see.

My God has never failed.
Grace and Mercy always prevail.

My God sits high up on the Throne.
He's in control; He's always shown.

My God has many promises.
I know there's not one I missed.

My God has this unconditional love.
He takes my heart and treats it like a Dove.

My God sees everything.
He knows just what blessings to bring.

My God sent His only Son.
He knew Jesus could be the only one.

My God held me today.
He kept me from slipping away.
MY GOD REIGNS.

April 9, 2009

Tear Drops And Rain

Tear drops and rain
Crying through the pain.
God is here my child.
It will only hurt for a little while.

Tear drops and rain
Camouflage trying to remain the same
Trying to remain sane.
It's just not the same.

Tear drops and rain
It's April showers hiding the pain.
While it's peace you're trying to gain.
God is keeping you close just the same.

Tear drops and rain
Will it put out the flame?
Will these showers
Bring May flowers?

Tear drops and rain
All wrapped up; this is no game.
Reaching out and no one is there
The rain showers fill the air.

God can you make it stop.
No more rain no more tears
Fill my heart with love
Take away my fears.

Tear drops and rain
No more pain
How great is our God
Wiping the tears from afar.
Joy has cometh this morning.

APRIL 17, 2009

Love Is Here

Love is here
Sent from above
I'm flying high
Like wings on a Dove.

Can't stop now.
There's so much to see.
God has given
New love to me.

I can't stop praising
I can't stop shouting
I'm even dancing
No more pouting.

The smile on my face.
It's real you know.
My pearly whites.
Have started to show.

Love is here.
Look, it's all around
I'm taking it all in
I'm no longer bound.

This is such a great feeling.
This is such a great Joy.
I've kept my eyes on the prize
Loving God even more.

Love is here.
I dreamed it would come.
God made me a promise
And He sent the right one.

One day it will be
Your turn to be free.
And open your arms
It's for you and me.

Yes, Love Is Here
With God's Blessings in tow.
It's ok for the whole world to know
So go ahead, let your love glow.

April 24, 2009

Letting Go

Today is Thursday, May 7th and as I entered a new level on my journey I thank God because He has let me see so many things. As I am rolling through my journey setting new goals, I am aware how the adversary is upset. He no longer steals my joy or peace. The car is gone and as I was cleaning out all my things, God is letting me see the greater "Treasures" that await me in Heaven. I never thought there would be this much peace in letting go and letting god.

As I travel along this journey, I have grown to appreciate the silence, my alone time with God and most of all, His Love. That is something no one can take from me. I am excited about the "NEW" God is going to send; I am excited about the closeness of my relationship with Him. One thing I would share today if you are separated or divorce, just remember "How Great God Is." He is keeping me, preparing me and most of all protecting me through it all.

Why Be Bitter

Why be bitter
About the past?
So it didn't last.
God is still there.

Why be bitter?
Things are better.
Counting on God.
He's true to the letter.

Why be bitter?
Life goes on.
New beginnings are here.
There is plenty to cheer.

Why be bitter?
It's a negative energy.
Let there be peace.
Positive thoughts can't cease.

Why be bitter?
It's not in God's plan.
Everything is in His hands.
Let Go and Let God.
PEACE!

Walking With God

Walking with God on this journey
I've come to realize how strong I am.
Never thought I was so tough
Even when the roads got rough.

Walking through the highs and lows
Sometimes wondering which way to go.
I never doubted my Lord and Savior
I knew I still had some divine favor.

Walking some days in the rain and with pain
He even showed me what I had to gain.
Respect and love were shown to me.
What ever the level I was to see.

Walking some days with blind folds on
Not knowing the answer I was torn.
Move those mountains I had to do.
My Lord was right there cheering me through.

Walking with God it's nothing new.
I'm His child, I wasn't through
Walking with God; right by my side
Giving me the power to continue this ride.

My journey is almost over.
I couldn't have made it by myself.
Walking with God, No He was walking with me.
He carried me, He couldn't let me be.

MAY 14, 2009

GOD IS ENOUGH

God is enough for me
Anyway I look at it.
It's Him that has set me free.

God is enough for me.
He's taken my mind
Uncluttered my thoughts
Just so I could cherish what was bought.

My salvation one Friday
Upon that tree
Way back on Calvary.
God is enough you'll see.

Gave us eternal life.
Peace and Joy.
God really is enough.
Can't ask for anything more.

God is enough.
Don't need that material stuff.
Treasures await in heaven one day.
Jesus blood has paved the way.

God is enough for you and me.
His faithfulness is what we need.
Walk in your victory, Stand fast to you goals.
Then one day, face to face, we will behold.

May 17, 2008

It's For Sale

The sign went up and people came to see
This house for sale among the trees.
God is doing His thing on this journey of mine
And very soon He'll find a new home for me
As I walk into my new destiny.

House For Sale

There is a house for sale
Down here on earth
But it will not compare
To God's Heavenly Turf.

I'm not putting much stock in this house for sale.
For a very long time more sadness did hale.
It hasn't been a home; nothing in it was mine.
I know God has something a lot more Divine.

A home filled with love.
Some peace and some joy
God would welcome you all.
Yes, this house is for sale and I'm standing tall.

May 20, 2009

Where Will I Go

While the house is on the market
I've been wondering where will I go.
Will I head South where the weather is warm
Or go North towards the snow?

A new home in a brand new place.
I feel the joy coming over my face.
I'm all packed up and ready to move
Waiting for God to approve.

It's exciting this part of my journey
How time flies it seemed an eternity.
All the highs and lows and the uncertainty
Seems forever towards my destiny.

Where will I go when this old house is sold?
I've asked God, but it's not been told.
I know he has something waiting with my name on it
And I'm not worried not one little bit.

For I know the plans He has for me
Moving me into my destiny
So much Joy, so much Peace
It's all waiting to be increased.

May 25, 2009

I'm In Love

Jesus is His name.
He doesn't play games.
True to His word.
Oh yes, and faithful too.

He knows just what I need.
I only have to ask Him once.
He comes to my rescue.
I never have to leave Him clues.

He promised to never leave me
And when I need to, He'll let me be
Giving me all the quiet time I need
Planting and sowing seeds.

He's been after my heart
Right from the start.
I've been playing hard to get.
Some days I really gave Him a fit.

Forgiveness never runs out.
He loves me without a doubt.
I love spending time with Him.
Of all the men He's a special gem.

Yes I'm so in love with Jesus.
My travel partner these past months
Sent the bubble wrap to cushion my bumps
Praising, praying and packing over the humps.

This great love of mine
Is shared by so many, how divine
I'm not the only one in His life.
He has enough for the world to share His light.

So join me in this awesome affair.
Jesus will always be there
Loving you, loving me
I can't think of anyone else I want to see.

May 26, 2009

A House Is Not A Home

As you look around your house
Is it a home filled with love?

As you look around your house
Does laugher fill the air?

As you look around your house
Are the decisions that are made, fair?

As you look around your house
Are family and friends welcome?

As you look around your house
Is the light forever glowing?
Is the Word forever showing?
Is Christ in every room?
Are you sharing, is there caring?

As you look around your house
Is it your Home?

May 27, 2009

SHE'S STILL FAMILY

It's June 12, 2009 almost one year into the journey and tonight I had the best conversation with Mama ever. We talked and cried and in all our years together we only had one argument. That was one too many. We spent hours in her kitchen in Ypsilanti canning, making jelly and peach cobbler. We told each other tonight that we will always love each other. She still wants me to come to help make jelly.

I wrote this poem for her at the beginning of my journey. It's 3:15 AM and she is on my mind. This year she will be 97 yrs.

MAMA

Hair so Fine
White as Snow
Sitting in her easy chair
Always on the go.

Canning corn from the cob
Cutting up peaches too
All for her family and friends
It is a big to-do.

If you ask her how she's doing
She'll comment fair to middling
And don't you try to stop her
From moving about and piddling.

She is busy in her garden
Putting through the house.
She really never made a fuss
Grabbing rags to remove the dust.

Working her big print puzzles
Every-night at dust
While making sure that all was right
Before she said goodnight.
June 12, 2009

At Last

At last the tears are gone
At last I'm almost home.
At last my new destiny is near.
At last there is no more fear.

At last the stars shine bright.
At last my future is in sight.
At last the garden blooms.
At last there's no more gloom.

At last my heart feels warm.
At last there is no storm.
At last my God has heard.
At last it was His Word.

At last my eyes do shine.
At last I feel Divine.
At last my praise is felt.
At last I'm glad I knelt.

On bended knees I thank you God.
For preparing me with your unconditional Love.
Holding me tight throughout the night
At Last we won the fight . . . I'm Yours.

June 19, 2009

This is one of those nights I wish my Dad were here helping me through this journey.

Thank You Daddy

Thank You Dad for all you've done.
I remember Fort Smallwood and all the fun
We had cook-outs and parties too.
Going for Sunday drives you always knew.

How you loved all your girls
Telling us about our pretty curls
Taking care of us through thick and thin
Never once did you give in.

Always there to dry our tears.
Comforting bad dreams and all my fears
Taught me how to change a flat.
Telling me you knew I would be back.

Thank you Daddy for the memories.
I miss you so much, yes we all do—
Patricia, Sandy, Terry, Maxine
And our angel in heaven, Anita too.

THANK YOU DADDY

June 29, 2009

My Praise In Packing

How do I decide what stays or goes?
Putting it in a box for me
Or should I leave it and let it be?
Not everything will fit into my new destiny.

Some things I haven't used for years
Saying to myself, "and why are you saving this?"
Letting it go to bless someone else.
My trash has become the treasures on their shelves.

As I pack, I pray, as I pray, I praise
It makes my day feel a lot less haze.
God made it clear to me,
This is all a part of His plan you see.

I've had you in this bubble wrap
Keeping you safe from all that crap
Protecting you day and night
Making sure you are in my sight.

I guess I'll be packing until I move out
Praying and Praising without a doubt
Knowing that when times get tough
He'll whisper, My child you're a diamond in the rough.

June 23, 2009

I'm Ok

I'm ok with God's plans.
I know that I'm in good hands.
Guiding me throughout the day
So much to do so little to say.

I'm ok on my journey he gave.
It's for freedom He paved the way.
Even the highs and the lows
He made sure I kept my glow.

I'm ok praising and packing
No one but me and God
Looking back to see how far
I'm becoming His shining star.

Yes, I'm ok through all my days
Keeping my joy and peaceful ways.
Talking to Jesus and listening too
I knew God was seeing me through.

I see the journey is almost near
I'm ok, my thoughts are so much clear.
Whichever way my God leads me
It's all good, I can't wait to see.

June 24, 2009

One Year Ago Today

I started this new journey
One year ago today.
He walked out of my life
And went about his way.

God was there to comfort me
Telling me now that I am free.
Self-esteem and confidence were restored
While God was opening new doors.

Friends came from far and near
Suddenly my destiny became clear.
Jesus was rocking me to sleep at night.
I never stopped praying, everything was all right.

Sometimes the road would get a little rough
But my Lord and Savior let me know that I was tough.
He wiped my tears and calmed my fears.
I realized just how He has always been near.

Yes one year ago today
I was on my way
To becoming free and more remarkable.
With God I knew all things were possible.

July 1, 2009

Brand New Heart

I never cared much about material stuff.
Sometimes I would shop and come home with nuff.
I don't buy just to have.
Most of the time there is nothing in the bag.

The gifts that were given were not from the heart.
I always knew it, right from the start
Things can never replace time or love.
It has very little meaning when it's not from above.

The house is sold and so is the car.
It never really took us very far.
When your heart is not in the place you called home
Don't waste your time; God has more than He's has shown.

My peace I give to you my child.
Open your heart and let's tarry awhile.
Stay close to me, I'm taking you somewhere
And don't ever give up or be in despair.

There is Love after Love.
A new home waiting for you.
There's laughter and treasure
And it's just for your pleasure.

So open your heart and your arms too
There is so much that God wants you to do.
He's been waiting a long time for your season to start
He has given to you
A BRAND NEW HEART.

JULY 3, 2009

Divine Downtime With God

Divine Downtown is where God has me
Holding me close to Him so I may see
All that He's doing in and through my life
Taking me new heights, delivering me from strife.

Divine Down time I'm in the den
But it's ok God hasn't left me,
Making and molding my destiny,
Getting me ready before He sets me free.

In my downtime I'm learning to stand still
Waiting for God to tell me the next move
Blessing me with divine favor and more
Giving me the confidence if I have to stand more.

He's fighting the battle; every one He's won
Because peace of mind is better than none.
He said you are almost out of this fight.
Just hold on; I'm giving you back your life.

Divine Downtime I've been told to hold on.
Just look at where you and God have gone.
Through hell and high water it's part of His plan
Making me strong with each hand.

Divine is the only way God does things.
Even during the times you don't understand
Just hold on to the promise that you know is yours
And watch when it's over; He'll be opening many doors.

So when my Downtime is over
When God say it's time
Don't ever look back
Divine Favor is mind.

July 24, 2009

How Do You Say Thanks?

How do I say thanks to those that I love
You have been on this journey with me like a Dove.
Showing me your love, encouraging me through.
Little did I know how much the family grew.

You loved me from the start, giving me your heart
Letting me share, and in return I found a brand new start.
I wrote it down through tears and fears.
It helped me heal and grow beyond my years.

My poetry didn't always make sense
To those who read and took offense.
It was never meant to hurt, just to vent.
My story, and at the end it was God who got the Glory.

So how do I say thanks to all who have shared
Encouraged and stood by me; you were there.
I only have my love to share from my heart
I hope you stick around for my new start.

I LOVE YOU WITH MY WHOLE HEART.

July 25, 2009

Because He Loves Me

Everything I have is because God loves me.
All the trials and joys that come my way
It is because I love Him each and everyday.
So I'll keep on praising Him in all my ways.

Because He loves me I can face tomorrow
Taking to Him all my pain and sorrows
Watching Him restore all that's taken
Never again will His love be mistaken.

Because He loves me my soul is rejoicing
He restored my soul and there is no forcing
His blessings are there and I am aware
Because He loves me and I know He's fair.

Every place I've been around the world.
I'm telling of His abundance grace and love.
Because He loves me it's easier to share
That eternal life is yours if you care.

Everything I feel, It's because He loves me.
On this journey His love has never ceased.
I'm giving Him all the Honor and Glory.
It's because of Him, I can tell my story.

Aug 2, 2009

Feelings Just Feelings

I feel God is trying to tell me something
Talking to me all day long in the right ear.
It's the miracle side only he can speak into.
I feel God is taking me somewhere I've never been.

I feel God is trying to take me somewhere.
I am following, there's no despair, He's got my cares.
I feel God has His Angels working overtime just for me.
Right now he can't leave me alone, He won't let me be.

I feel God is working it all out His way.
Be steadfast on this journey is all He has to say.
Stay true to yourself, stay true to your faith.
Stay true to Your God while he makes a way.

I feel this and that, I feel out of the mess.
I feel wonderfully made, I feel a lot less stress
I feel I'm in His arms. I feel no harm.
I feel God all over my face, this place, this race.

I feel you God, I'm all wrapped up in Your Arms.
Thank you God, I FEEL YOU.

Aug 5, 2009

Love Is The Key

As I look into your eyes
Listening to your words
Smiling in your face
Wondering if we are in the right place.

As I listen to your words
As they roll off your lips
Piercing my ears as I listen,
Praying what you're saying isn't.

As we talk throughout the night
Learning about each other
Making promises, making plans
Holding each other's hand.

Putting Christ in the center
Quoting Scriptures in the air
What a comfort we are there.
Is it too soon to share our hearts?

He is our Shepherd. He will guide.
Letting go, taking it in stride
No need to slow it down; it's OK.
Love is the Key, God is having His way.
But now abideth faith, hope, love, these three; and the greatest of these is love.
1 Corinthians 13:13 NIV

August 13, 2009

Where's My Song?

There's a song in my heart today.
It speaks a sadness that I cannot pray.
I'm trying to think where this melody is from.
I can't give this song any more room.

There's a song in my mind
That I cannot find.
It is hiding and I can't get a grip.
Lord please don't let me slip.

I hear the music, I can't feel the words.
I need your guidance today Lord.
What have You heard?
Let the music play, no not today.

One day the music can be so upbeat.
The next day the sound is defeat.
Where is my melody, where are the notes?
My song, I can't let it go.

I'm reaching out to you.
Oh my Lord, let everything that has breath
Sing, make a joyful noise, praise the Lord.
Let the harps play; It's my song It's my day.

There's a song in my heart today.
It has a melody that floats in the air.
As I sing and I praise, God it making a way
For that special song in my heart today.

I will not let the music die.
I will not let my melodies be defeated.
There is a song, God's song in my heart.
Not just today but every day, Sing Girl Sing.

August 17, 2009

Just Another Silly Love Poem

Just another silly love poem
That's in my heart today
Inspired by God, Nurtured with love.
It only can be sent from above.

Just another silly love poem
Keeping the laughter in my heart
Know God has placed it all.
Before I got my start.

I didn't know how He was going to use me
To share this silly love
But aren't you glad I'm sharing
About how our Savior is so caring?

Is this really a silly love poem
Or is a silly person sharing love?
Coming out of the box today
Laughing, hugging and sharing, that's her way.

No, it's not a silly love poem.
It's not a silly thought
Because when she started writing
She was serious about your heart.

August 18, 2009

LITTLE GIRLS AND PANCAKES

This morning I needed to get out the house and think about the good old days. Today is August 22, 2009, so I called my Mom and told her I was coming over. She said she was going to make herself some "Pancakes" and asked me if I wanted any. Well, I said no but when I got there the house was smelling so good, I said "Mom, I've changed my mind, Yes give me a plate of "PANNY CAKES." She laughed and said she hadn't heard that word since we were little girls.

LITTLE GIRLS

When I was a little girl
My Mom made breakfast for all.
The skillet was hot and ready to make
A big stack of her Panny Cakes.

There were six of us, my Mom & Dad
And there was so much love to be had.
Four little girls with many curls
Waiting for their breakfast of Panny Cakes.

The plates were full
And the blessing was said.
Everyone was really glad
Panny Cakes for breakfast we all had.

I Need You Lord . . . Right Now

PSALM 91

Right now I need you Lord
to come into my space.
All the arrows are flying
And headed for my face.

The adversary is busy
Plotting; he's up all night
And when the daylight comes
He is all up in my sight.

I'm on my knees daily Lord
Thanking You for Grace
But when the adversary comes
I need a hiding place.

I need you Lord right now.
Just put me in your arms.
You have to keep protecting me
From those who do me Harm.

September 1, 2009

A Grateful Heart

Right from the start it took my heart
To know what's right from wrong
Although I may fall from standing tall
It was Jesus Blood who paid it all.

A grateful heart that's been repaired
No more days of being in despair
My God has turned it inside out
Making it pure without a doubt.

There were times when I could not see
All that Jesus meant to me.
My heart was far removed from the light.
I prayed daily that God would bring back my sight.

Sight to see the Glory of it all
Sight to see that I can stand tall
Sight to see and feel His love
Sight that came from Heaven above.

A grateful heart with love to share
A grateful heart that really cares
A grateful heart my savior protects
Making sure there will be no more neglect.

The days go by quickly you know
And God has cleared all that's unwanted.
He has put in place this grateful heart
And has taken it to a brand new start.

September 8, 2009

Show Me Lord

Show me Lord the direction to go.
Tell me everything I need to know.
Keep me strong on the path you have chosen.
Love me and comfort me so all of it shows.

Show me Lord what work needs to be done.
Tell me Lord how I can help everyone.
Keep me focused with the job before me
Giving You all the glory to see.

Show me Lord; forget me not.
You're keeping all your promises and I haven't forgot.
I'm still in the bubble wrap waiting to be shipped
Into my destiny that you have equipped.

Show me how Lord just a little peek
Of the future I can't wait to seek.
Beautiful dreams they come at night
Telling me it's going to be all right.

Thank you Lord for showing me the way,
Thank you Lord for giving me a new day,
Thank you Lord for keeping me sane,
Thank you Lord for all that I've gained.

09/12/2009

HE HAS MY HEART

Right from the start
Jesus had my heart.
He kept it safe for me.
Then one day He set it free,

Free to make some choices
Listening to many voices,
Standing back so I can choose
Making sure His love I'll never lose.

He has my heart in His hand
Giving me the strength to take a stand
Standing for righteousness, standing for love
He's teaching me the meaning of.

The meaning of joy, patience and kindness,
The meaning of meekness, long suffering
Faithfulness, goodness, peace and gentleness
And the meaning of self-control, keep holding.

Jesus keep holding my heart,
Keep guarding and keeping it safe.
My love for you is growing still,
My heart in your hands is real.

September 14, 2009

ONLY MY GOD

You might have seen it in our blogs
OMG so many people have logged
But when I looked at these letters today
It said something else, so I'll like to say.

OMG has a ring of its own.
I'm going to change it to a new tone.
ONLY MY GOD, That's what it means.
OMG will be different the next time it's seen.

Only My God has never failed.
Only My God we are the head and not the tail.
Only My God can you find refuge in Him.
Only My God treats us as a very special gem.

OMG is here for you.
Trust in Him to see you through.
You are precious in his sight.
So OMG, love Him with all your might.
Only My God has never left my Journey.

September 18, 2009

LOVING YOU

Loving you is easy.
You are so close to my heart.
You cleared out my life
And gave me a new start.

The journey, your plan
Footprints in the sand
Carrying me through.
I loved you, you knew.

Loving me so unconditionally,
Me praising You, my amazing God
Loving you with all my heart.
I'm patiently waiting for my new start.

I love you, it's so easy to say.
I can't believe I'm on my way.
A way you have made for me
Thank you God for setting me free.

Free to be me, free to see
All the beautiful things inside of me
Standing tall, chin held high
Taking my dreams beyond the skies.

Yes, I'm loving you.
Only My God knew what to do.
I'm so glad for this time with you
Wrapping, Packing, Praising, I'm new.

09/22/2009

The Night Jesus Found Me

The night He found me I was curled up in bed
All sort of stuff was going through my head.
I looked to the left and I looked to the right.
And I heard Jesus saying, fight with all your might.

He found this little girl in a world of her own
Not wanting to come out, just leave me alone.
I will not leave you a strong voice I heard.
I opened the door and said not a word.

As he put His arms around my lifeless body
I trembled and shook and cried out with pain.
He rubbed my face and said to me
My child you have so much to gain.

You have come a long long way.
Never look back, hear what I say.
You are stronger and wiser and so beautiful inside
Keep taking your steps towards your great prize.

The night Jesus found me I'll never forget
The Love and Compassion I was glad that we met.
The cost of my pain in my own little box
It was Jesus my Savior just saving His flock.

09-23-2009

A New Home

A new home is waiting for me
I don't know where but I can see,
A home filled with love and peace
God is preparing and my praying won't cease.

A new home with all that I prayed.
The walls will be blessed before I get to stay.
There will be laughter, praise and joy.
I couldn't have asked for anything more.

A new home that's what I dreaming about.
God will make it happen I have no doubt.
There will be trees and flowers in the garden to see
Somewhere to sit where I can be free.

I can see it coming very soon.
I can sit on the porch and watch the moon.
The stars will shine bright above the yard
And I won't have to go very very far.

So I'm taking this moment to thank Him in advance
Singing, Praising, Dancing, yes it's my chance.
I appreciate the Blessing He wants me to see
For my new home God will send just for me.

Sept 27, 2009

Heaven Must Have Sent This

Heaven must have sent this.
We didn't have a clue.
Isn't it amazing
How things worked out for you?

His hands are on my life
There's angels all around.
The blessings they keep coming.
New Joy and Peace I found.

Heaven must have sent this.
How else can I explain
Why favor falls upon me.
I have so much to gain.

He walked this journey with me.
Some days I could not see
The blessings He had waiting
Are just about to be.

I know heaven sent this.
The pain, the joy, the light
God wanted me to see it
Before He gave me life.

Heaven sent this love
And I'll cherish it every day.
He's walking right beside me.
My God has made a way.

10/14/2009

My Secret

I'm happy,
An attitude of gratitude
Following my dreams.
Joy is mine it seems.

I love being me.
The world will see
My mind is filled with peace.
I am a possibility.

I will achieve,
Writing only to please
Deserving much happiness
Feeling God's Blessedness.

I have been prepared,
To sing my song,
To write my story
And giving God the Glory.

The power is in me
For all of you to see
God's love I'll keep
Cherish the moments that I seek.

I feel good right now
Knowing that He's here
Loving me so much,
I'm so grateful for His touch.

10/15/2009

This Is Where I Am

This is where I am:
Peace, love, joy I feel
Thinking positive thoughts
It's all been revealed.

Loving and lovable
Finally making it happen.
Sun is shining on rainy days.
I'm seeing it all come my way.

Blessings are full.
Favor is mine
Feeling all of God's favor,
Grace divine and so much more.

10/16/2009

FEELINGS

These feelings are trying to come.
Don't let them in, it's no fun.
I went to a wedding today
Maybe that's why I'm feeling this way.

I've asked God for so much lately
Giving me the desires of my heart
All within His will.
I just have to get through these chills.

Some days are better than the others.
Letting go and letting God
It sure will make you wonder
Why this occasion took me under.

I'm trusting God to get me through.
He's done it before because He knew
I would have days like this.
That's why God has never missed.

10/17/2009

LOVE FOUND

Is love ever really lost
No matter how it's tossed?

Is "I love you" loosely stated?
How would you rate it?

How many loves do you have
How many loves has gone bad?

Does love have limits?
Or are your feelings timid?

Strong love never fails.
Failed loves don't prevail.

When is it love?
When does it turn to hate?

Is love faithful?
Or are people unfaithful?

Is love pure?
Or people impure?

Love found, love lost
At what cost?

October 26, 2009

JESUS, ARE YOU HERE

Jesus are you here
because there isn't no more fear.
Dark days are gone
And so are the storms.

Jesus are you here?
There are so many things more clear.
The love you have for me is one.
Thank you for being a faithful Son.

Jesus are you here?
I'm feeling your touch
I need you so much.
Jesus are you here?

October 30, 2009

IF I WERE NOT HIS

If I weren't His I would be lost.
It doesn't matter that He's paid the cost.
My life would be in limbo, my dreams shattered.
If I weren't His not much would matter.

I would be wandering about
Like a little lost sheep
Never really feeling
His love that's so deep.

If I weren't His my days would be weary.
Everything I see would be distorted and blurry.
My heart would be heavy and the days would be long.
I would have no idea where I belong.

If I weren't His the sun would not shine.
Everyday would be cloudy and I would be in a bind.
No joy, just pain would take over my life.
All it would be is misery and strife.

But that's not the case as I sit here and write
Thanking Him for all the gifts that are in my sight.
More blessings are coming every day and night
Because I am His everyday of my life.

11/10/2009

Keeping His Spirit With Me Through The Journey

It was a warm sunny Sunday on that November 18, 2001, that the Lord called him home. I remember telling him on that Saturday... "Daddy, I'll be back tomorrow to watch the football game with you." I kissed Him good-bye, told him that I loved him and that was the last time I saw him. My heart still Hurts, I miss Him so much. I know if he were here during this past year of my journey, he would have called me every day. He is my Hero, My Daddy.

February 19, 1923-November 18, 2001

Eight Years Ago Today

Eight years ago today
You made your way to heaven.
Didn't say goodbye
Just spread your wings, took off to fly
Just headed for the open sky.

I know you went to a better place.
God was waiting in all His Grace.
He looked at you with just a glance
Said well done; now here's your chance
A chance to see all the loved ones there.

And although I miss you so very much.
Your smile, your laughter and even your touch.
I'm glad you're with the Father today.
I'm glad that He still makes a way.

I MISS YOU DADDY

November 18, 2009

Love Came, It's Time To Say Goodbye

Love came years ago.
It wasn't right; we did know.
Played this worldly game
That caused some hurt and so much pain.

Love came; we made it right.
Asked for forgiveness; then took flight.
Somehow it never was smooth.
We just couldn't find our groove.

Love gone after so many years.
I know I'm done shedding tears.
He's moved on and so will I.
I'm trusting God as I say Goodbye.

12-02-2009

HOME SWEET HOME

This week I moved into my new place.
God has put a smile upon my face.
I know it was sent from above
Beause God has already filled it with Love.

It's small and quaint, just my size.
I just couldn't believe my eyes.
Home Sweet Home, My new place
Filled with His love and so much grace.

A place just for me
Favor and blessings it was meant to be
Thanking and praising all day long.
My heart is filled with a brand new song.

Home Sweet Home.
That's where I'll be
Making new memories.
Yes, God and me.

12/28/2009

NEW YEAR NEW JOY

It's a New Year.
There's a new joy.
I have conquered my fears.
The tears are no more.

It's a New Year
An exciting time.
Jesus said all would be mine.
It's a New Year.

It's so true about your joy.
Just keep asking your God for more
It's a New Year; sing praises to Him.
So much in store is about to begin.

It's a New Year.
New joys, new peace.
Grace and Mercy are always there.
Pray without ceasing; God really cares.
IT'S A NEW YEAR.

01-07-2010

Just Thinking

Just thinking about all I've been through
Just thinking about how great is our God,
Just thinking about my children,
Just thinking about the friends that stayed,
Just thinking about the friends that left,
Just thinking about all the prayers I sent up,
Just thinking about all the prayers that were answered,
Just thinking about the prayers that weren't,
Just thinking about grace & mercy,
Just thinking about how He kept me safe,
Just thinking about my family,
Just thinking about my Dad,
Just thinking about how fearfully & wonderfully I am made,
Just thinking about how this journey showed me just how strong I am,
Just thinking about the gifts & talents God has allowed me,
Just thinking about how blessed I am to live here.
Just thinking about my new destiny.
Just thinking about how much Jesus sacrificed for me.

01/16/2010

Thoughts And Prayers Through My Journey

A Journey Through Thoughts and Prayers

I feel so blessed and loved. I love you God. I just wanted to express that right now.

I'm on this new journey and I can't wait to see what God is going to do. I've always depended on people for almost everything. Today it feels good to depend on God.

I love the way He is taking care of me for such a time as this. Unconditional love, grace, mercy and peace.

JUST BREATHE . . . I'm going through, I need hope, time out, Deeper faith, higher praise. Just breathe, I know God is still here with me.

MANY THANKS AND MUCH LOVE 08/07/2008

    They say you never know who your friends are until something happens. I found that to be true during a number of occasions throughout my life. I think of the many trials I have been through as an adult before I got saved and after. Of all the trials I've been through I found this to be truer during past few weeks. Many of you who will read this will know what I'm talking about. Today I feel blessed because I realize just how much I am loved, respected, and wanted. My friends and most family have been very supportive, caring and loving. It has given me a new outlook on why the trials. If we didn't have trials we wouldn't know how big our God is and how He "Fixes" them. Without trials we would think that we are in this all by ourselves and nobody cares. My trials helped me to grow.

Tonight I thank God for this special time in my life to get to know Him and to share with real people my heart and my love . . . Tonight I want to thank you all for your love.

Remarkable & Strong Terry

RIDING WITH GOD 08/14/2008

This week I turned off my radio in the car and devoted my ride to work talking to and listening to God. I've prayed, confessed, laughed, cried and yes I was even silent. What I know for sure, it is the best part of my day. When I walk into the office I am so covered I glow. I can handle everything and what I can't handle can wait until I can, God got this too. When I leave the office I am ready for the latter part of my day whatever He sends. I am stronger not because of anything I've done but because of who He is in my life. I Love Him So much.

ANOTHER LEVEL OF GLORY

08/23/2008

As I sit here and write what's in my heart I can't help to look back seven weeks ago when I thought "Where is God?" I thought why it is so cold in July. I wondered if anyone can see my anger, can anyone feel my pain, does anyone hear my cries. I was screaming out for help, going in circles, staring into space. This interruption, these trials, seven weeks, a brief moment, God was up to something.

Tonight I randomly opened up my Bible and turned to Psalm 116. Awesome God, I was just thinking how He is hearing my cries on this journey. Psalms 116:1-19 **1** I love the LORD, because he hath heard my voice [and] my supplications. **2** Because he hath inclined his ear unto me, therefore will I call upon [him] as long as I live. **:3** The sorrows of death compassed me, and the pains of hell got hold upon me: I found trouble and sorrow. **4** Then called I upon the name of the LORD; O LORD, I beseech thee, deliver my soul. **5** Gracious [is] the LORD, and righteous; yea, our God [is] merciful. **6** The LORD preserved the simple: I was brought low, and he helped me. **7** Return unto thy rest, O my soul; for the LORD hath dealt bountifully with thee. **8** For thou hast delivered my soul from death, mine eyes from tears, [and] my feet from falling. **9** I will walk before the LORD in the land of the living. **10** I believed, therefore have I spoken: I was greatly afflicted: **116:11** I said in my haste, All men [are] liars. **12** What shall I render unto the LORD [for] all his benefits toward me? **13** I will take the cup of salvation, and call upon the name of the LORD. **14** I will pay my vows unto the LORD now in the presence of all his people. **15** Precious in the sight of the LORD [is] the death of his saints. **16** O LORD, truly I [am] thy servant; I [am] thy servant, [and] the son of thine handmaid: thou hast loosed my bonds. **17** I will offer to thee the sacrifice of thanksgiving, and will call upon the name of the LORD. **18** I will pay my vows unto the LORD now in the presence of all his people, **19** In the courts of the LORD'S house, in the midst of thee, O Jerusalem. Praise ye the LORD.

24 HOURS; LESSONS FROM MY HEART

On August 27, 2008, I spent 24 hours in the emergency room. Tuesday while getting ready for work I experienced severe chest pains. After the third sharp pain I drove myself to the hospital with what I thought was a "Heart Attack." They draw blood every few hours to check your eczemas and that's what I want to talk about.

The first four tubes of blood they drew were dark red, alm*ost* the color of "black cherry" instead of "cranberry." So I asked the tech. why my blood was so dark, I've never seen it that color before. About three hours later the same dark cherry color. The next few draws were also dark. In the meantime I had a cat-scan and an echo of the heart, even a chest x-ray. They kept me hooked up to monitors and continued to observe me, all the test came back negative for a "Heart Attack."

God spoke to me and said, "My child, your heart is being attacked by the enemy." The next two draws of blood were bright red, the color I'm used to seeing. God was showing me something.

The Sunday before I went to the hospital I went to church, my spiritual hospital. There I heard two magnificent sermons with wonderful praise and worship in song. God had sent me to The hospital so I could see the sermons that were preached on Sunday. How awesome is that!

I went to the hospital with my heart under attack by the adversary. God removed that tainted blood from my veins. The entire test came back negative. God was working this thing and by the end of the evening my blood was covered by His blood and had returned to its bright red color with the reflection of His grace and mercy. While there are some things I have to do both spiritually and medically, I am grateful for the lessons learned in the "Emergency Room," God's Hospital.

Thoughts of Thanksgiving

As I think about the last five months on my Journey, one day of Thanksgiving just isn't enough. I have to look back at all the days when there was only one set of FOOT PRINTS in the sand and I thank God for carrying me through those days.

I also have to thank God for the Angels He sent by way of phone calls, fellowships over a meal, many cards and yes, even the Internet. As my journeys continue at this new level I have to give thanks to God for the strength He has given ME. I have to Thank Him for the relationship that we now have. I have to Thank Him for the transformation and joy.

Oh I still have those "Not so Good Moments" that sneaks into my day, but I can't help but praise Him in those times too. I know it's nothing but satan coming to try to steal my joy, he tried last night but My God and I got the victory.

Awesome God, that's what I have to keep saying to myself over and over and over again. If we just look around and feel His presence, give Him thanks and praise then we will have His peace, joy, love and blessings.

More than once I've heard my Pastor preached this in his sermons over the years:: "Lord take it off my heart like you put it on my heart. I had no idea how powerful this prayer was until I prayed it one night. Amazingly it works.

Let not your heart be trouble, Ye believe in God, believe also in me. John 14:1 KJV

11/30/2008

My Remarkable Journey

It's December 10, 2008 and while everyone is getting ready for the holidays, I sit and reflect on how my life has changed. God has set my life on a brand new journey. From July 1st I have shared with you parts of this Journey but today I am sharing the personal side of this Journey. God has bought me a mighty long way. I am looking forward to spending time with family and friends and meeting new friends, discovering the new me in Jesus and setting personal goals. This year I can't wait to celebrate Jesus birthday and mine.

MERRY CHRISTMAS MC FAMILY

12/12/2008

    This has been a wonderful year even with the highs and lows on this journey. On my journey I have been blessed with a network of family that have loved, prayed and encouraged me. I am so thankful that God has places you in my life for such a time as this.
    I am looking forward to 2009 with great hope that God is going to do wonders for all of us. I see healing of relationships, marriages, families and friends. I see new beginnings for others as well as myself.
    God is so amazing and His grace and mercy are everlasting. He is faithful and just. I never thought my relationship with the Lord could get better but it has and I'm still growing. I have been talking to Him a lot lately. He is the reason for my transformation on this journey and I am so grateful.
    I like to wish my MC family a Merry Christmas and a blessed and peaceful New Year. Love and hugs

I Am A Remarkable Woman

It's January 6 and as 2009 came in, I began to reminisce about 2007 not 2008. In January 2007 I began a program with sixty women from my church called "Becoming A Remarkable Woman." When I started the program I wasn't sure if I would even finish. I had been beating myself up, didn't like how I looked, what I weighed and had low self-esteem. I thought of excuses from Monday through Saturday and thought, "why not to go to church on Sunday". My prayer life was the pits and my Bible just sat on the table waiting for me to pick it.

I remember telling my class of thirteen women that this was my last chance and if it didn't work I was "DONE." Well praise be to God, I finished the program, won the Butterfly award and thought I was on my way to a fulfilling relationship with my Lord and Savior; it didn't happen.

It was in the middle of 2008 that the Remarkable Woman program kicked into my heart and life. It was then that my self-esteem and confidence begin to soar; it is now that my love and relationship for God and my joy have returned. The joy that I am experiencing was like in 1985 when I first joined church. I was on fire and ready to learn.

I have had many prayer partners and mentors in the past six months and they have all been a real blessing to me, praying, Encouraging and offering good Christian advice.

My peace, my praise, my joy, my God is real. It's been a long time coming. I am moving mountains. This joy comes from God. As long as I have breath I WILL PRAISE THE LORD.

God's Love Is The Key

02/01/2009

February is the love month and to me it starts from the first to the twenty-eight. As I sit here and think about love, my favorite scripture comes to mind.

For God so loved the world, that he gave his only begotten Son, that whosoever believeth on him should not perish, but have eternal life. John 3:16

Of all the Valentine cards from the past none offered me this kind of love. The love God had for me that he sacrificed His only Son to die for my sins. That's love.

God wanted us to know just how great love is so He gave us 1 Corinthians 13:13 But now abideth faith, hope, love, these three; and the greatest of these is love.

If God thought the greatest ever was love, why can't I. Is it because of the past hurts caused by man, family or friends? Could it be that I can never feel real love until I developed an intimate relationship with God?

There's an old school song that asks, "What's Love Got To Do With It?" Well, everything. God gave it to us in the Ten Commandments, more than once. Love your Mom & Dad, love your neighbor, love the Lord you God. He commanded us to love.

John4:7 Beloved, let us love one another: for love is of God; and every one that loveth is begotten of God, and knoweth God. **8** He that loveth not knoweth not God; for God is love.

WOW, here's a scripture telling us "God Is love." I spent years trying to find the true meaning of love and here it is. Right before my eyes. Jesus loves Me This I Know, Cause The Bible Tells me So. The Bible tells me God is love. In the King James version the word love appears 131 times in the Old Testament and 179 times in the New Testament. That's 310 times all together. I think God mentioned it so many times so that we could get it. God I got it.

Update on God's Goodness

02/23/2009

I have to give God the all honor, the praise and the Glory. He is working this thing out, has His arms wrapped around me and I can't move without Him but then again I don't want to be without Him. I'm keeping my mind stayed on Him, throughout the process. A wise friend told me "HE" was all I ever needed and now I know that for myself. I've learned most of my lessons the hard way and lost some friends in the process but God is faithful. On this journey while I have not been easy to love, made a few mistakes, my true friends will always be there and for that I'm grateful. This Scripture was given to me a few weeks ago by Mrs. C from church, a friend and mentor. Thank You, I appreciate you so much. To my family and friends thank you for your messages, poetry, comments, encouraging words and prayers, I appreciate you.

Your personal concerns for me have blessed me more than you'll ever know. My Remarkable Sistergirls, love you much, thanks for keeping me busy. My kids are awesome. God is amazing.

GOD AND BUBBLE WRAP

It's March 12, 2009, and I'm talking to God. He's been keeping my company while I'm packing up what will go with me on my new journey and helping me let go the "stuff" I will sell or give away that will have no place in my future.

Some days I pack while talking or listening to God and some days He just takes over and does it all. There is a lot of bubble wrap here but I see something greater in the wrap. You see we wrap our precious stuff in bubble wrap that we don't want to get broken while being shipped.

So today I looked at all this bubble wrapped around the house and said "that's God." He's all wrapped around me, I'm His precious cargo. I've been "Shipped" along on this journey for nine months and not once did I break. Oh I had some moments when I cried, had panic attacks and screamed but I didn't break. That's because God (bubble wrap) had me protected for shipping through my journey.

I will continue to praise, pray and pack. God and plenty of bubble wrap. The box marked "Fragile Precious Cargo" will arrive at its destination soon.

My Journey

It's now February 9, 2009, and I've been on this journey for eight months and eight days, but who's counting? I've had some highs and lows. The greatest high has been my relationship with God, great because he restored my joy, praise, peace and my soul. He has given me back my self-esteem and freedom. I'm listening, hearing and focusing on Him and His Word.

I've met new friends and old friends are reconnecting and God is in control. My dreams are being thought about again and my smile, well what can I say but thank you Jesus for all that You have done. I'm trying to let go my anger by picking up a pen and God has given me some great things to write.

I don't know why February was chosen as the "Love" month because when I think of love and my heart, It's like a heat wave, more like August than February. (Smiles)

At this very moment my thoughts are with my sister Maxine and through our years. I'm so glad God made us sisters.

2009 was supposed to be my year of "Moving Mountains." Well I've moved some and some are still there. My faith at times really shines and when it doesn't God has my back. As this phase of my journey draws to a close, I have so many people to thank who's been here with me so far. I appreciate you.

My Journey, God got this. Amen

In Case I Don't See You....
Goodmorning, Good Afternoon
& Goodnight... June 17, 2009

I have so much I would like to say but I'm so tired right now. I am so overwhelmed from the "busyness" of today. I'm going to spend the next few days writing, reading, relaxing and praying. I must return to my "Bubble-Wrap" and finish praising, praying and packing. My prayers will be with all those in need and everyone gets a "HUG." You have blessed me tremendously and I appreciate you so much.

Friends~Lovers~Marriages

FRIENDS
They come into your life with smiles
Having fun, laughter sometimes across the miles
Sharing a dinner or two, making plans for something new
Not knowing what the future holds and oh how the friendship grew

LOVERS
Time went on and their was talk of love.
You kept wondering if it was sent from above
Asking God is this the one as you continued to both have fun.
Maybe this could be a lifetime thing so you went out and bought a ring.

MARRIAGE
On bending knee one day, you push aside what you wanted to say.
You let God guide you through this time of planning, He knew just what you'll be saying.
I love you with all my heart; please let me make you an important part.
Come into my life and share my world. With God all things are possible for our new start.

August 6, 2009

A Smooth Transition

It's January 26, 2010, and moving from a house to an apartment was easy. I spent the week-end still letting go of stuff that I packed and bought with me only to find that there is absolutely no room for it. Again I had to decide what to keep and what to let go. When I was in my home it was easy giving away everything. As I saw truck loads of furniture, home accessories and collectibles drive out the driveway I knew it was going to a better place, homes where my belongings will be appreciated. I was letting go a past and a life that I shared with someone.

The amazing thing that happened today was I took three bags of "Bubble-Wrap" to my church to use to pack up for our upcoming move to the new church that is being built. Today I heard on the news that "Bubble-Wrap" turned 50 years old and I thought about the beginning of my packing to move and how God "Cushioned" me in His arms, protected me like "Bubble-Wrap" and as I moved along the bumpy roads of my journey I did not break. How awesome is that.

So I continued to "LET GO AND LET GOD" giving away the old and bringing in the new. New furniture, new accessories and making new memories, I can't think of anything else but praise and thanksgiving for how far He has bought me. I WOULD NOT HAVE MADE IT WITHOUT HIM.

It's Friday, February 5, 2010, I signed my divorce papers. I have no idea what God has for me on my new journey in my new destiny but I have opened my heart to HIM to receive all that is within HIS will. I have started my new book of poetry with a brand new outlook on life. As I'm leaving the courthouse it is snowing, so white and so pure as I start my new journey.

A Big Snow Storm Is Coming My Way

There's a big snow storm coming my way.
I went to the market in the middle of the day.
The market was crowded and the parking lot too.
Why is everyone making such a big to-do?

The baskets were filled with all kinds of junk.
You would think that we'll be stuck for a month.
I got very little and went on my way.
I don't think the snow will be much to stay.

So when this big snow dumps on my town
It will be awhile before we see the ground.
I am excited because I missed the first one.
Went down south that day to visit my son.

With so much to do inside of my place
I will cherish this time, thanking God for grace.
I don't have to worry about getting bored
Because there's still some boxes all over the floor

So be safe everyone if you have to go out.
This is the big one without any doubt.

God And The Mailman

The mailman came and bought my letter.
It confirmed that my life would be better.
It was only three pages for me to read.
It was all I needed, I had been set free.

God is amazing, so full of love.
He makes no mistakes
And sits high above.

Jesus, His Son paid for it all
Died on the Cross; He took the fall.
God delivered just like the mailman
Setting me free was His master plan.

2-26-2010

I'm Glad I Was Wrong

Whatever I thought was going to happen on my journey didn't happen. God proved me wrong. He was faithful. He never left me. He provided ALL my needs.

I stood still and got to know God and it was not easy. There were many moments of anxiety, tears and doubt. There were many prayers, words of encouragement, phone calls and visits from family and friends.

God knew whom to put in my life on this journey and He knew whom to take out of my life during this journey and I'm grateful for both. For whatever God laid on your heart to share with me, thank you. I have appreciated each and every one of you.

Writing has been healing but the time I've spent with God and His Word has been the biggest comfort on my journey towards peace and joy.

Last but not least

Writing this book has helped me to heal in many ways but more importantly it has helped me to let go and grow closer to God. I have accomplished so much during the past three years on my journey that has been so amazing. I'm praying you have been encouraged and inspired to write a journal so that eventually you'll find the peace that God has for YOU. With God all thing are possible.

For I know the plans I have for you," declares the LORD, "plans to prosper you and not to harm you, plans to give you hope and a future. Jeremiah 29:11, NIV

It was for freedom that Christ set us free; therefore keep standing firm and do not be subject again to a yoke of bondage. Galatians 5:1

To God Be The Glory